NOT THE PERFECT BOOK

A Perfect Personal Development Guide For Not So Perfect People

By
JW RUCKER JR

Disclaimer

All the material contained in this book is provided for educational and informational purposes only. No responsibility can be taken for any results or outcomes resulting from the use of this material.

While every attempt has been made to provide information that is both accurate and effective, the author does not assume any responsibility for the accuracy or use/misuse of this information.

This book is dedicated to:

My Wife Adrianne and my Daughters, Yolanda, Naomi, Ariel, and Ariana. Fond Memories of my Dad Joe Willie Rucker Sr. Who always taught me to "keep it moving"

Introduction

Congratulations on your purchase; I pray this book will become an effective tool for you to use in all of your future and present pursuits. I must give full disclosure before you continue. This is not the perfect book ...

- For those who choose to judge and cast stones.

- For those who choose to allow negative thoughts to dominate their life.

- For those who choose to follow the status quo.

- For bullies who promote hate and fear.

However, this is the perfect book for those who dare to dream, favor wisdom over folly, are guided by belief and faith, and understand that there is more to life's story.

This book is designed for those who would like to create a better version of themselves in the areas of leadership, relationships, self-confidence, compassion, faith and decision making.

This book is also a study guide, journal, and workbook. That will enable the reader to actively participate in writing a personal prescription for success that is authentic only to him or her.

Our bodies and minds are constantly in a state of vibration. Vibration is a law that governs transmission and reception. As transmitters we consciously and subconsciously broadcast thoughts and emotions. These thoughts and emotions do not remain invisible. Oftentimes thoughts and emotions become visible for all to see and hear. This is why the heart (conscious thought) and mind must be guarded at all times. These are our most valuable assets that few put little value on.

Position yourself to receive continuous waves of positive vibrations that work towards your purpose. Be mindful of your goals/plans at all times. Seek wise counsel from those who are of similar mind. Surround yourself with people who have reached the level of success that you are working towards. Demand wisdom from the Infinite power that resides within you. Speak Aloud to yourself (when you are alone) in repetition; this will help reprogram the subconscious mind.

When you begin to complete the interactive lesson pages, the contents are for your eyes only. It is always best to keep your "Billion Dollar" ideas to yourself until you start to put those ideas into definite action. This book is a guide, connecting philosophical principles and divine laws based on our human condition as it's foundation.

For best results follow the steps outlined below.

1. At the end of each chapter/lesson there is an interactive action plan. This is designed as a self-evaluation. Each evaluation will provide a snapshot of your current thoughts related to your personal/authentic success. When the completed lessons are combined a big-picture view and framework will manifest to either add to or begin written plan to obtain the good that you desire.

2. Take your time. You will be unpacking new information and dissolving old habits. It is quite possible that you will discover new things about yourself.

3. Do not procrastinate in completing the lessons

4. The doorway to your 'authentic success' is faith. Keeping an open mind, it is essential.

5. Have a well-defined and determined purpose (DDP)

6. Write, record, playback, and read. Make sure this is done daily to repeatedly impress your new thoughts and ideas upon your subconscious mind.

Lesson One: Success

Did you know, success is a word that is stamped in the foundation of the human experience without regard of context. According to Google, 'success' originated from the Latin word succedere which means 'come close after'. In the course of time (16th Century) the word transformed to the word we know today. The word gained popularity within the framework of the bible translations commissioned by King James in the 16th Century A.D. A popular scripture that contains the word is from the book of Joshua Chapter 1 verse 8

"This book of the law shall not depart out of thy mouth; but thou shalt meditate therein day and night, that thou mayest observe to do according to all that is written therein: for then thou shalt make thy way prosperous, and then thou shalt have good success."

Success is now defined as a favorable outcome, prosperity, profit, affluence, wealth, riches, and fortune. The known opposites of success are poverty and failure. The meaning of 'success' is straight forward. However, what does it mean to you? Well defined goals that are acted upon with diligence are in themselves successful. One has to learn to stop and recognize and be grateful for the small successes that are leading to the desired goal. These goals/plans should be written with breath (flexibility) and made personal (authentic).

In our human experience there could be people that measure their success by someone else's goals. This method of achieving success can be stifled if one does not have goals of their own. However, there is a difference when one can adopt points taken from the success goals and plans from another and integrate those goals into their own.

Get on The Starting Line

Are you in shape to run the race? If so, get on your mark. If you are not ready much preparation is in order. This race is either won or lost in the mind.

"No man is ever whipped until he quits in his own mind."
-Napoleon Hill

Lesson Guide (download full lesson guides from https://bit.ly/omrworksheets)

1. What do you know about success?

_____

2. What do you want to know about success?

_____

Chapter Discovery/Key Takeaways from this chapter.

New Ideas- write down 5-10 keywords that will trigger new ideas about your success path.

_____

Return to this chapter in 3-5 days, write down what you have learned about your success path.

Repeat the following affirmation at least 3 times a day.

I am successful in doing the good that I desire to do. Because I am one with the source of all that is good to which I am forever grateful. -JW

Lesson Two: Rendering Services

Do unto others as you would have them do unto you. - Luke 10:27

Pray for those who despitefully use you-Matthew 5:44

Do not be weary in well doing for in due season you will reap an abundant harvest if you do not give up. -Galatians 6:9

From fortune five hundred companies to selling goods out of the trunk of your car. One has to always be mindful how services are rendered and the perceived value of the service or services you render. Providing a service in a negative state of mind can quickly put a rendered service out of business. Napoleon Hill writes, "It should be encouraging to know that practically all the great fortunes began in the form of compensation for personal services, or from the sale of ideas."

To accumulate fortune, one must first see and practice that first sale in the mind. Part of one's daily plan should be the daily practice of visualizing a conversation or conversion before the workday begins. When Visualizing, there must be an attitude of friendliness and humility. To know yourself is to know and understand the power that resides in you. Life experiences, gives each individual on this planet glimpses of what happens when our minds (the superconscious subconscious and conscious) align with the one principle source of power. A great example is when a person receives an unexpected sum of money or favorable news.

One should know and understand that these are not random happenings on the part of the universe. These are thoughts that were visualized at some point in time and manifested onto our plane of existence. For some of us, this happens on a consistent basis. However, for most it is hit or miss. The reason why is because each individual who is a part of the human condition has been programed with degrees of indifference towards situations, people, and things. One must learn how to overcome these indifferences to receive the results you desire.

Indifference of any kind can hinder your progress. A good suggestion to help rid yourself of this success crippling emotion is to write them down and analyze them objectively one by one and begin to dismantle them by replacing them with positive thoughts. For example, some people are indifferent to money. And their favorite saying is "money isn't everything."

Most of the time the people who say this are indifferent towards people who earn or have a substantial amount of money through their vocation or occupation. This attitude will keep you from achieving the success you desire. Remind your subconscious mind that...

"money is an idea in the mind of God, and it is good and very good."-Joseph Murphy

Tips:

- As a rule, the person offering his or her service must be in a positive state of mind in the presence of potential clients and customers.

- Learn how to sell yourself by asking leading questions. Do not get drawn into arguments over unimportant things. This is a distraction that will zap your positive energy.

- When you feel angry or agitated learn to pause the moment by taking a deep breath and smile. This simple move will trick the subconscious mind and take it out of the default adversarial mode. Then gracefully remove yourself from the situation.

- Realize that we are selling all the time. Convincing your wife why you should have an RV. Or your wife explaining the benefits of having an expanded closet.

JW Rucker Jr.

Affirmation:

> *"Today I choose the best idea for myself. I know that as I build a high idea of myself that I will draw to me all that I can conceive and I conceive of new and exciting things for me to be to do, and to have."*-F.K. Eikerenkoetter

Lesson Guide:

1.What do you know about rendering service?

_____

2. What do you want to know about rendering service?

_____

Chapter Discovery/Key Takeaways From This Chapter.

New Ideas- write down 5-10 keywords that will trigger new ideas about how you render your
service.

_____

Return to this chapter in 3-5 days, write down what you have learned about your rendering quality service.

JW Rucker Jr.

Lesson Three: Your Calling

The pursuit and landing of a desired career could take some time. However, while you are waiting on your "dream job" one probably settles for what I call a 'steppingstone position.' This is definitely not the time to have thoughts of frustration. According to The Balance Careers.com website. "The median number of years that wage salary workers have worked for their current employer is currently 4.6 years. Then, according to the Bureau of Labor Statistics it appears that "job hopping" is a trend among young people in their thirties. People who are in management positions remain in those positions for five years or less."

Imagine if your vocation (what you are called to do) can be merged into your career. This would eliminate your version of the typical 'job' from your current mindset. Eventually the word job and its typical visions that are conjured by the subconscious will not be a part of your daily conscious activity.

On the other hand, some people favor organizations that compensate them on a scheduled basis according to their work experience and their ability to perform a task that is required for the advancement of that organization. Some people see this scenario as a win-win experience because they believe they are working in their calling.

Having a definite and defined purpose (DDP) is what everyone should have as he or she enters a situation where earning money is the main objective. Knowing your calling is not enough. A plan must be put in place for long-term success. This plan must be revisited and revised consistently with contingencies in mind.

For those who are "satisfied" with their current occupation, there is always a possibility of the organization/system they are employed with downsizes, closes completely, is taken over, or suddenly seeks a younger staff. Another scenario could occur were the individual has a life change in such a way that She or He can no longer perform the tasks that most organizations require.

It is safe to say that either of the above scenarios can have a devastating negative impact upon an individual. If the person is responsible for heading a household the damage will ripple through everyone that resides in the home as well as other people, the person is associated with.

An esoteric exploration of the bible story of Job can relay one's feelings when everything is going well then, a sudden change of life occurs. Towards the end of Jobs' story, his emotional rollercoaster came to its climax when the Infinite source of all power confronts him for the first time with these words "Gird up your Loins." or prepare to strengthen oneself for what is to come. However, it could be taken as "Stop moaning and put on your big boy or big girl pants.

There is more to you than meets the eye. One must realize that everything originates from your thoughts. A vocation can make a way for you. However, this takes desire, persistence, belief, and faith.

Private and public failures or what we perceive as failure happens to every human being on this planet at some point in time. Again, if you have a written plan or goals make them flexible, available for change, and

read them often.

Tips:

- One must purposely and consciously believe that he or she is worthy of their calling regardless of their past.

- The perfect outcomes that originate from not so perfect circumstances always start with keeping your end desire in front of you.

- Get rid of all negative thoughts. Your subconscious mind can play them in a continuous loop that manifest unwanted feelings and emotions. If you are not aware that these emotions are damaging, they will appear normal and will delay or stop your progress.

- Take time to discover and determine your true place within your current occupation

- Do not compromise your values or beliefs or feel indifferent towards new ideas.

- Beware of weakness of desire. When you begin to procrastinate on your plans and goals.

- Do not fear criticism from anyone including family.

Many people make mistakes in relationships be it personal, private and within their careers and vocations. These people go through life unhappy and miserable because she or he fear criticism. However, what the person fails to realize some criticism in the form of wise counsel can

JW Rucker Jr.

help that person think differently and place their progress on the right track.

Napoleon Hill writes, "Too many people refuse to set high goals for themselves or even neglect selecting a career because they fear the criticism of relatives and "Friends" who may say "Don't Aim So High, people will think you are crazy."

Affirmation:

Right here and right now I am in my true place doing what I want to do. Being who I want to be and having what I want to have. My vocation is making a way for me and all who I come in contact with me. Today I feel the happiness, love, peace, and joy, that is divinely granted to me.

-JW

Lesson Guide:

1.What do you know about your true calling?

_____

2. What do you want to know about planning to work in your true calling?

_____

Chapter Discovery/Key Takeaways From This Chapter

New Ideas- write down 5-10 keywords that will trigger new ideas about how plan to work within your true calling.

_____

Return to this chapter in 3-5 days, write down action steps toward your long-term vocational plans.

Lesson Four: Knowing You

It is hard for the ego to allow a person to admit their weaknesses. Oftentimes one struggles to keep up appearances just to hide a weakness. In the context of holistic leadership, a person must always self-analyze to confirm and transform any thoughts, emotions, and actions that could harm themselves and others.

An Inscription found in the ancient temple of Apollo at Delphi reads "Know Thyself." Knowing who you are is the first step to success. Coming to grips with and consciously purging bad habits, false imaginations, indifference and self-doubt may be difficult to confront during this step of the process.

In my book & weekly podcast Align: Living Life on Purpose, I discuss the power that the subconscious mind has over an individual. Popular belief tells us that we only utilize 10% of our mental faculties. However, Modern science confirms that 95% of our day runs on the default programs of the subconscious mind. From breathing to bad habits, we are subject to those programs moving from invisible to visible on a daily basis.

When one is quiet and still, we can communicate with our subconscious through conscious repetition of positive affirming and visualization all of this must come with feeling. This combination will help to record over the things you no longer want to come out of your subconscious. The famous bible verse from the book of Romans chapter 12 starting at verse 2 reinforces this concept.

Knowing yourself, is not a reason to ignore others or the positive vibrations others can bring towards you. You should know yourself enough to recognize when the universe is trying to deliver what you want. Gut feelings, daydreams, and out of the blue occurrences should not be ignored. Your conscious mind must be open and aware of these occurrences. The great thing about this is that you have a choice to ignore and give in to your regular programming or purposely and cautiously follow the prompts that you are provided.

JW Rucker Jr.

Affirmation:

"By day and by night I prosper in all of my interest."-JW

Tips:

- Every thought presents a cause. Focus on the good you would like to see in yourself and others.

- Never use terms like 'I don't,' 'I can't,' 'I hope,' maybe, or try.

- Honestly evaluate yourself as often as you can. Download the I Can Checklist and negative self-talk evaluation questions to get started. (https://bit.ly/selfevalomr)

Lesson Guide:

1.What do you know about you?

_____

2. What do you want to know about how to effectively and purposely reprogram negative habits and thoughts?

_____

Chapter Discovery/Key Takeaways From This Chapter

New Ideas- write down 5-10 keywords that will trigger new ideas about how to work beyond the default level of the subconscious.

_____

Return to this chapter in 3-5 days, write down action steps toward your long-term plans on improving your conscious awareness.

Lesson Five: Connections

The close connection between leading and following is obvious. However, there are misconceptions that they are entirely different. A leader is an influencer just as much as a follower. Both labor together in symbiosis. When that relationship aligns, the two become one. The one source of universal power is revealed in all of us. This infinite energy cannot be created or destroyed. The beautiful side of this is that we all have the ultimate connection.

This is documented throughout the human experience. For example, the book Genesis and the book of Exodus reveals this Principle source of power is the essence of all that is. The ancient saying below summarizes the relationship between the Principle Power and man.

"Ever the same is my inmost being, eternal, absolutely one, whole, complete, perfect, indivisible, timeless, shapeless and ageless without face, form or figure the silent presence fixed in the hearts of all men."- Joseph Murphy

Aligning with the Principle Power (God) with purpose and desire will attract those of the same mind. This attraction happens without much effort on the part of all of those who are aligned with the Principle Power.

Recognizing the laws of vibration and attraction provides one with the advantage of connecting with the right people, situations, and ideas that can bring prosperity and guide one to an abundant life.

As with everything, networking with others starts in the mind. Start to visualize people that you will see maybe in an upcoming meeting or on your daily walk as happy, and friendly. When you send out this vibration before you it will fill your path with receptive people who will return your vibration to you with a warm and friendly smile.

In a spiritual sense, your thoughts are angels that you can command to fly through the universe without the limit of time and space to act on your behalf. However, programmed thoughts that we may be unaware of are continually passing back and forth in the universe and

JW Rucker Jr.

when these thoughts manifest in our life's they can be positive or negative. This is what I call hit or miss.

How do you see yourself right now? The primary connection must be with ourselves. What do you see when you look in the mirror? Can you look at yourself without judgement? When you can connect with yourself without judging your looks or your past deeds you can begin to see and feel the person you desire to be.

The great leaders that we have come to know in this human experience, always expressed the concept of self. These leaders always implied or stated their relationship with the Principle Power. These leaders also recognized and understood the laws that govern the universe.

What many may consider supernatural, enlightened humans see it as a normal way of life. The story of how a carpenter from Nazareth demanded the elements we know as wind and water come into alignment with the Principle Power by declaring peace and demanding the elements to be still.

As the story goes the former carpenter turned ministry leader asked the ship's crew why they were so astonished when he calmed the storm. It was as if Jesus was saying that anyone with enough faith and knowing who they really are could have done the same thing.

You have to believe that you are a part of a whole universe that is designed to serve you. To acquire a clear understanding of this story I suggest you read the book of Luke chapter eight verse twenty-two thru twenty-five.

JW Rucker Jr.

Tips:

- Great people understand the power of connection. Believe that after you study this concept you will be able to recognize and apply the power of connection.

- Have a strong desire to move towards your vision.

- When connecting with others, visualize everyone with a happy attitude.

- "Your thought fused with feeling becomes a subjective belief. According to your belief it is done unto you."- Joe Dispenza

Affirmation:

I am in the principle life force and the principle life force is in me and nothing is impossible. -Joseph Murphy

Lesson Guide:

1.What do you know about connecting with other people?

_____

2. What do you want to know about how to effectively and purposely connect to like-minded people and positive circumstances.

_____

3. What have you learned from this lesson that you did not know in reference to connections.

_____

Chapter Discovery/Key Takeaways From This Chapter

New Ideas- write down 5-10 keywords that will trigger new ideas about how to open new positive connections in your life

_____

Return to this chapter in 3-5 days, write down action steps toward your long-term plans on improving your connections.

Lesson Six: Persistence

The history of our human experience is filled with success stories of those who were persistent in seeing that their invisible ideas or thoughts become visible. We are always reading about these people not realizing that we have a universe that is willing to provide you with all of the good that you desire. Napoleon Hill writes;

"As one makes an impartial study of the prophets, philosophers. "miracle men" and religious leaders of the past. One is drawn to the inevitable conclusion that persistence, concentration of effort, and definiteness of purpose, were major sources of their achievements."

A lot of successful people may not understand why there are those within our human experience that choose to give up when life takes for them take a negative or positive turn. It appears that what we are able to see in front of us is what we tend to react to, and the default programing of our subconscious mind takes over.

Seeking, asking, and knocking is not a religious concept. These are instructed actions that we should take in pursuit of our desires. This is done naturally when we are attempting to win the affection of another. However, when it comes to pursuing a career, vocation, car, house, etc. most often fail to follow the instructions all the way through because of distractions that happen along the way.

When one is in pursuit of anthers affections nothing stands in the way. There is a laser focus on the person that you want to share your life with. Now imagine using the same tenacity, emotions, and focus on the good things that you desire for your life.

Leaders must display and practice persistence because it leads to success. The vibrations emitting from your persistence will attract all of the components needed to bring a project to life. One must not fear failure but embrace it as a lesson and continue to persistently move forward.

JW Rucker Jr.

Revisit your written plans/goals, consistently. Document the how and the why of the failure and proceed to input new ideas. Consult with those who are in your success circle because sometimes they can see objectively what you cannot. When your new ideas are set revisit the plan consistently so that it will be impressed upon the subconscious mind.

It is documented that Henry Ford came from humble beginnings and he did not possess the degrees and diplomas that his legacy now a global industry requires from its employees today. It was Fords persistence and understanding of the human condition that catapulted him to fame and legacy.

Vehicles that bear his name are on and off roads around the globe. So, it is safe to say that persistence in the pursuit of a worthy idea can leave an inheritance for generations to come. Another example would be Thomas Edison who held a third-grade education. Lewis Latimer an African American collaborated with Edison on the invention of sustainable light.

It was Latimers' invention of carbon filament that keeps a light bulb bright for hours on end.

Mari Van Brittan Brown inventor of the home security system was a nurse by trade.

However, her persistence in pursuing her vocation created a legacy for her and her family.

Tips:

- Persistence has to have a defined purpose and strong desire.

- Written plans and goals must be revisited on a daily basis.

- Shield your mind from negative vibrations, negative thoughts of others, and distracting situations.

- Create a success circle of liked minded people.

Affirmation:

My Persistence leads me to abundant living for I am one with the Infinite.

-JW

JW Rucker Jr.

Lesson Guide:

1. What do you know about persistence?

_____

2. What do you want to know about persistence?

_____

3. What have you learned from this lesson that you did not know in reference to your personal habit of persistence.

_____

Chapter Discovery/Key Takeaways From This Chapter

New Ideas- write down 5-10 keywords that will trigger new ideas about how to increase your level of persistence.

_____

Return to this chapter in 3-5 days, write down action steps toward your long-term plans on improving your persistence.

Lesson Seven: Desire

What do you desire most right now? Is it good health? Is it happiness? Is it love? Is it success? Is it prosperity? Is it money? If you have answered yes to all of these questions, congratulations you are human.

The desire to control our own circumstances is embedded deep into human consciousness. You could say this was a gift that we inherited from the creator. Humans were given dominion over everything on this planet. Most importantly, we were given total control over our thoughts.

There is a plethora of human controlled systems that fight to control your mind. Overtime these human initiated systems began to study behaviors that are common to us all and learned how to manipulate populations for their individual benefits which are power and money.

You might disagree and say well "no one has power over me." You are right, no one has power over you unless you freely give in or give up. Programs placed in your subconscious mind since birth have helped develop your world view. However, some or most of those thoughts do not belong to you. They were originated by systems designed to keep populations of people from their true birthright.

To remove yourself from system's that are designed to project scarcity and lack has to be fueled by your desire to take control of your circumstance. This is done by changing the way you think. The bible and other ancient text hide the instructions on how you can take your control back in plain sight. I wrote more about this in my first book and I talk about it in depth on my podcast.

Having the desire to stand out among the crowd can lead to a life of abundance. Many people who think they are shy, or lack confidence can overcome those labels by reprogramming their subconscious thinking.

Being the "Black Sheep" is not a negative connotation as the world-mind would have you to believe. It means that you are going against a norm induced by the human condition. Divinity is your birthright. This includes good health, happiness, love, success, prosperity and money. To stand-out in a system of white sheep is to have the desire to live an abundant life.

There are many successful people that came before us and who are among us who were and are examples of what I call the "black sheep principle." These are the people who understood the divine laws of the universe. "Can any good thing come from Nazareth?" Were the words of Nathaniel in John 1:46 when he was told about a seemingly uneducated backwoods preacher who would later change the world.

There are many who were deemed as underdogs and black sheep that changed the landscape of our human condition. If you believe that your ideas or thoughts will not conform to those around you, mums the word until you find like-minded individuals who will understand the direction you desire to take.

Without the desire to change your conditions for the better you will continue to believe the world-mind instead of the invisible world of thought and vibration. It is the job of the world-mind to keep the masses

JW Rucker Jr.

distracted just enough to doubt themselves. "Be not conformed to this world but become transformed by the renewing of your mind."

These ancient instructions transcend time and space because the writer understood the human condition. These words were hidden under the guise of religion, but this statement warns us about world systems including religion.

What is your desire for your life and for those around you? Imagine the impact your ideas and goals will have on others. The worst thing that you can do is nothing. You were born with desire. As a child you imagined great things and as you grew there was no one there to teach you about the true power that we possess and how to use it.

De-Sire or "of the Father," means that your desires are spiritual in nature and deeply express true feelings.

Tips:

• Visualize (imagine) that you already have what you desire.

Not The Perfect Book

- Override or reprogram the subconscious mind by constantly reaffirming your true desires.

- Determine if your present emotions belong in your idea future.

- Be able to give thanks for a future that has not been made manifest yet.

Affirmation:

I am firmly established in Gods avenues of infinite ever flowing and overflowing supply. -Joseph Murphy

Lesson Guide:

1.What do you know about desire?

_____

2. What do you want to know about desire?

_____

3. What have you learned from this lesson that you did not know in reference to your personal desires.

_____

Chapter Discovery/Key Takeaways From This Chapter

New Ideas- write down 5-10 keywords that will trigger new ideas about how to increase your level of desire.

_____

Return to this chapter in 3-5 days, write down action steps toward your long-term plans on improving your true desires.

Lesson Eight: Faith

We always hear people say, "have faith." The human experience is predicated on faith. However, there are many people who lack faith. The reasons for this deficiency originate from one's view of his or herself.

In the human experience, there could be people who silently compare themselves to others and may for the most part feel that their life cannot measure up to those that have a proven track record of success in their personal and professional endeavors.

As I write this, our global community is mourning the death and celebrating the life of Kobe Bryant an American basketball player who along with his young daughter two of her teammates and their parents lost their lives yesterday in a fatal helicopter crash. Kobe entered professional basketball directly from high school. Although he had the physical stature of an adult player, he was still a David in a realm of Goliaths. However, he believed that he could conquer these basketball giants and his confidence (faith) in his own ability to do so launched a legendary career

and life for him.

I believe if Kobe would have compared himself to sports legends

that came before him and those who were in the league with him, he

would have diminished his own abilities. However, the human experience

reveals that faith can give one the courage to see, know, understand, and

execute their gifts without excuse or apology.

Varying world views and superstitions can condition one to believe

only what they can see and hear in turn keeping one from focusing on the

truth about the greatness that lies within each individual on this planet.

Keith Khan-Harris writes, "Just as we can suppress some aspects

of ourselves in our self-presentation to others, so we can do the same to

ourselves in acknowledging or not acknowledging what we desire." Faith

is the essence of your desires (the substance of things hoped for) that have

yet to be manifested onto our dimensional plane (the evidence of things

not yet seen). Faith is not your religious affiliation. Believing that you can bring your ideas of joy happiness and freedom into your experience can only come by faith.

There are many people who need help with unbelief. Mark chapter 9 verses 23-25 illustrates a perfect example of this issue of the human experience. A famous science fiction character says, "I find your lack of faith disturbing" A famous teacher from Nazareth would often say. "you have little faith." Why is the obvious so difficult to understand? Doubt, fear, and anxiety are enemies of faith. These also are perfect entryways for manipulative people, systems, and organizations to control your mind.

Negative emotions caused by fear, doubt, and anxiety are for the most part not warranted and are not based on total truth. The sub-conscious mind automatically starts to run the programs that it learned from negative past experiences and implanted superstitions and prejudices.

One way to combat this, is not to worry about 'how' certain events are going to happen and how certain circumstances will unfold. Once a person prays or affirm his or her thoughts with the one principle power that resides in them, that desire should be left with the infinite believing that it is already done. I call this the fire and forget method of manifestation.

Another work of faith is visualization. See your desire and believe you have it and it will come. This works when one is not monitoring time because time does not exist within the operation of the universe.

Tips:

- Feeling is the essence of prayer, see your desire, feel your desire, and believe you already have what you have asked for.

- Do not be concerned about the 'how.'

- Believe in yourself and the power of the I AM in you.

- Give thanks for already having what you desire.

Affirmation:

"I Am grateful for the One Infinite Power that lives in me". -JW

Lesson Guide:

1. What do you know about 'Faith'? (In your own words)

_____

2. What do you want to know about 'Faith'?

_____

3. What have you learned from this lesson that you did not know in reference to your personal view of 'Faith'?

_____

Chapter Discovery/Key Takeaways From This Chapter

New Ideas- write down 5-10 keywords that will trigger new ideas about how to increase your level of Faith.

_____

Return to this chapter in 3-5 days, write down action steps toward your long-term plans on improving your idea of 'Faith'.

Lesson Nine: Emotions

"Let not your heart be troubled" can be comforting words when one believes the world is against them. Doubt, fear, anxiety, and stress are oddities of our human experience. Ancient text and modern science reveal that human beings were not created to have these experiences. However, the world-mind manipulates the population to believe otherwise. The power of suggestion is very strong and when used purposefully and skillfully it can be used to enslave the mind and manipulate emotions forming a matrix of predictable and controllable outcomes.

The science of emotions proposes that keeping a good state of overall good health is essential to you achieving lasting authentic success in your life experience. We often hear the expression "it comes from the heart." According to science, the hearts electromagnetic field passes information of a person's emotional state throughout the whole body.

The rhythmic beating patterns of the heart changes significantly as different emotions are experienced. Anger and frustration are associated with erratic, disordered, incoherent patterns in a heart's rhythm. Love and appreciation are associated with a smooth and consistent pattern in the heart's rhythmic activity.

Emotions are described as "energy in motion." The psychophysiological alignment causes the hearts rhythms to show a sinewave (clean energy) like pattern and the electromagnetic fields become organized leading to higher and more positive emotional vibrations. It is amazing that all of this is happening in the realm of emotion.

"When you make the two, thought and emotion one. You will say to the mountain move away and the mountain will move away."- The

Book of Thomas

The previous quote is taken from the book of Thomas that focuses on the sayings of Jesus. It is safe to say that it is not our words that come out of our mouths in our time of prayer and meditation but our thoughts and feelings. Some people wait for things to happen outside of them to trigger a positive emotion. However, in this sequence emotions are like the firing, boom, and awe of fireworks. The emotion(s) fade away and the person is back to their default pre-recorded emotional programing.

The sequence must be changed. The joyful, happy, and peaceful emotions must come before the manifestation. One has to feel and believe that it has already happened. This will attract what you desire to you. Establish the mental equivalent of what you desire, and the result will follow. The price for this is believing that it is already done and by faith it will manifest into your experience.

The state before sleeping and just after waking is when your brain is in 'theta.' Theta is the frequency pattern the brain resonated during the first seven years of your life. This is when the subconscious is recording and not playing. Repetition will manifest the experience if you visualize and feel a sense of well-being and thoughts of peace. Thoughts are the electric charge (vibrations) and feelings are the magnetic force that align with the One Infinite source of power.

Tips:

- Practice deep breathing. There are many guided meditations on social media that you can start with until you are comfortable doing it on your own.

- Start with a 17 second visualization before bed and in the morning before the start of your day. Build on this by increasing your time at our own pace.

- Take time to do something that makes you happy.

- Warning, negative emotions can have a negative impact on your biology. Often with a delayed effect.

- Only you can make you angry, love, happy, sad etc. You have control over your emotions.

- Read and understand the instructions in Jerimiah chapter 17:7-8 as it relates to human emotions.

Affirmation:

"I AM What I want, and I attract what I AM" -JW

Lesson Guide:

1.What do you know about 'Emotions'? (In your own words

_____

2. What do you want to know about 'Emotions'?

_____

3. What have you learned from this lesson that you did not know in reference to your own...

'Feelings'? _____

Chapter Discovery/Key Takeaways From This Chapter

New Ideas- write down 5-10 keywords that will trigger new ideas about how to increase your frequency of producing positive emotions.

_____

Return to this chapter in 3-5 days, write down action steps toward your long-term plans on improving your emotional state.

Lesson Ten: Your Subconscious Power

Ancient text reveal, how each generation in our human experience explored the workings of the human mind. This chapter will offer a cursory overview of mind exploration with an emphasis on the "subconscious" and Its relationship with the One source of Infinite power. The purpose here is for you the reader to explore and research this vast subject so you can make an informed and purposeful decision about your life and how to live it in abundance.

In the context of "mind exploration" the word (mind) appears in the Christian bible 92 times. And other ancient text reveal that not understanding our minds relationship with the One Source of Universal Power could be detrimental to our individual life experience.

"And it is not for any soul to believe, except by the leave of God, and He lays abomination on those who have no understanding." **(Quran 10:100)**

*"It is a man's own **mind**, not his enemy or foe, that lures him to evil ways." "We are shaped by our thoughts; we become what we think. When the **mind** is pure, joy follows like a shadow that never leaves." ***(Gautama Buddha)**

JW Rucker Jr.

*"I The Lord search the heart and examine the **mind**, to reward each person according to their conduct, according to what their deeds deserve." (**Jeremiah 17:10 NIV**)*

Many years before the Greeks, the ancient inhabitants of Kimet (Egypt) studied the workings of the human mind. And how to control its behaviors. (Check out the story of the Tower of Babel in Genesis 11:1-9 and explore how it relates to the mind.) The studies of Imhotep and other Nile Valley scientist and philosophers predate the works of Aristotle, Plato, and Hippocrates.

New discoveries in space and in the depths of earth's oceans cannot begin to compare to the wonders of the human mind. Sigmund Freud presented the terms "subconscious" and "conscious" around 1893. Neuroscience tells us that the left hemisphere houses the conscious mind which screens incoming stimuli and acts as a gatekeeper for the subconscious in the right hemisphere, which is the non-critical pattern-oriented component of the brain.

Religious superstitions, limited beliefs and negative sayings handed down through our family trees can be dissolved when individuals start to ask questions and have a desire to make informed decisions about how His or Her own mind operates.

The modern teachings of Prentice Mulford, Dr. Bruce Lipton, Frederick Eikerenkotter II, Joseph Murphy, Napoleon Hill, Dr. Joe Dispenza, and many others have produced a plethora of experience and information about the power of the subconscious mind. However, in its totality, humanity and its daily experiences have yet to scratch the surface.

The United States Government has commissioned military branches to study the power of the human mind. Unclassified CIA documents (https://bit.ly/docCIAomr) regarding the "Gateway Process" reveals how the human mind can produce and perform "miraculous feats." There exists a Universal Source of Power, the One Infinite source that every entity be it celestial or terrestrial in the known universe is connected to regardless of dimensional appearances. (1Corinthians 15:40).

The "world-mind" uses organizations, print, radio, social, and visual mediums to promote fear and insecurity in the form of scarcity, pestilence, glamour, and chaos, which for some cause anxiety, depression, fear, and self-doubt. Shunning, abandonment, and embarrassment are some of the tools that seemingly benevolent organizations will use to keep their participants in spiritual and mental slavery.

There have been and are now many "Masters of Mind" that have tried and are trying to teach the masses how to truly be free and live in abundance. This was the truth of the message the carpenter from Nazareth shared with those of his time. However, it is safe to say that the message has been distorted by vain traditions and unnecessary religious practices.

Thoughts become things. Look around you. The tablet, smartphone, or computer your using to read this study originated in someone's mind or maybe a collection of "like minds." You too can produce something that will have an impact on our human experience. The Henry Ford's, Albert Einstein's, George Washington-Carvers, Elijah McCoy's, and Nicola Tesla's aligned themselves with the One Divine Power that resides in them. Alignment with the Infinite brings about definite purpose that trigger positive changes to one's life experience.

"The divine exercise of self-knowledge, which ultimately enables man to live in happiness and in harmony with the divine laws of God, is based primarily on a careful study of the special relationship existing between man and the Universe."

-Rev. Willie F. Wilson

Manifesting your desires into your experience can be done consistently once you realize that you were born with the power to create. The "brick wall" most people run into, are limited beliefs and superstitions about having all the good things that one desires. Understanding that you have a power in you that has a direct connection with the One universal source is the beginning of true mental and spiritual freedom.

There are cultural and generational ideas that promote misguided judgements about people who have the desire to achieve or who have already achieved a level of material and spiritual success. This "world-mind" uses these 'misguided judgments' as a tool that keep those who conform to the status quo in bondage. The One universal source of power

JW Rucker Jr.

has instructed humankind through those who understand its laws, not to be conformed to this world (the world mind) but become transformed by the renewing of your individual mind. In other words, learn to think for yourself. Do not handover your creative authority to those who do not have your best interest in mind.

To affirm is to state that it is so, and as one maintains this attitude (believes its true) regardless of what is happening externally you will receive an answer to your prayer. In other words, your desire is your prayer. Condition your mind that your life is a constant prayer. Prayer without a definite purpose, with judgement, and hidden motives cannot be answered. These negative elements violate universal laws.

Your affirmation succeeds best when it is specific and when it does not produce a mental conflict or argument. For example, affirming you have a certain amount of money may conflict with a thought that has been programed in your subconscious mind. Instead of affirming a specific amount, it is simpler and more acceptable to the subconscious to repeat words like 'wealth' and 'success' three to four times a day for 5 minutes at a time.

Changing your mind is not easy because change upsets the status quo. When it comes to the mind; old habits, limited beliefs, and generational superstitions will fight to remain where they are unless you purposely and consciously make an effort to change it. Remember we are running in default mode at least 95% of our day. The subconscious is running your body based on past experiences and emotions. You are only conscious about 5% of every waking day. The good news is, the subconscious can be reprogramed to give you the life experiences you desire.

Tips:

- Be careful of self-doubt, this can lead to self-sabotage of your desired life experience.

- Commit to discerning the "world-mind" and its ability to use the power of suggestion to hold unsuspecting persons in mental and spiritual bondage.

- Shy away from negative news. Those vibrations can trigger your subconscious to activate past negative emotions that can have an overall effect on your physical health.

JW Rucker Jr.

- Know and understand that the One Infinite source of power lives in you and you are worthy of all of its love.

- Research and study information related to the workings of the subconscious mind like the works of Dr. Joe Dispenza, Dr. Bruce Lipton, Napoleon Hill, and Joseph Murphy

Affirmation:

The energy of the Infinite Power animates and sustains me. Creative ideas unfold within me, revealing to me everything I need to know. -Joseph Murphy

Lesson Guide:

1.What do you know about the subconscious mind? (In your own words)

_____

2. What do you want to know about your subconscious mind?

_____

3. What have you learned from this lesson that you did not know in reference to your personal view of the subconscious mind?_____

Chapter Discovery/Key Takeaways From This Chapter

New Ideas- write down 5-10 keywords that will trigger new ideas about how to reprogram your subconscious.

_____

Return to this chapter in 3-5 days, write down action steps toward your long-term plans on improving your ability to manifest your desires.

Epilogue/Conclusion

Persistence, definite purpose, planning, having connections, and providing your service, does not have to be perfect for you to succeed. However, these things should be driven by your desire to believe in what you are doing and the great things that you are capable of inside and outside of the world's unreliable definition of "perfection". With this process of thought, you can literally renew your mind overnight.

Your emotions are energy in-motion and wherever you focus, that energy can manifest "things" in your outer environment and even affect your biology at the cellular level. If your thoughts are negative stress and anxiety occurs. In contrast, if your thoughts are consistently positive gratitude and peace will keep you in a high vibrational frequency and you will attract the good that accompany those vibrations.

Using, meditation, affirmations, and self-evaluation are the tools that you can use to carve your-self into the person you desire to be. Exercise, healthy diet, and good sleep habits all start from thought and understanding that there is not one "perfect" solution that exist. Everything should be customized to fit your lifestyle.

This workbook is designed to help to get you started on the journey. The worksheets are made for self-evaluation and discovery of new ideas and thoughts that can help you improve performance in your business and personal pursuits.

In addition, I invite you to join community www.alignurmind.com , Our You Tube Channel **Align:U** and the podcast **Align Living Life On Purpose** to receive Free...

- e-books

- articles

- videos

- audio files

that connect with the subjects of Law of attraction, nutrition, exercise, business, stress and anxiety and much more at no cost to you. Consider this as a food supply for your journey.

Write a review on Amazon and Share your thoughts about this guide. It will be much appreciated.

JW Rucker Jr.

Bibliography

Boyczuk, Robert W. *The Book of Thomas*. ChiZine, 2012.

Dispenza, Joe, and Daniel G. Amen. *Breaking the Habit of Being Yourself: How to Lose Your Mind and Create a New One*. Hay House, 2015.

Eikerenkoetter, Frederick. *Rev. Ike's Secrets for Health, Happiness, and Prosperity--for You!: a Science of Living Study Guide*. F. Eikerenkoetter, 1982.

Hill, Napoleon. *Think and Grow Rich*. CreateSpace Independent Publishing Platform, 2017.

The Holy Bible: Containing the Old and New Testaments Translated out of the Original Tongues and with the Former Translations Diligently Compared & Revised. American Bible Society, 1986.

Kahn-Harris, Keith. *Strange Hate: Antisemitism, Racism and the Limits of Diversity*. Repeater Books, 2019.

Lieberman, David J. *You Can Read Anyone: Never Be Fooled, Lied to, or Taken Advantage of Again*. YLP Publications, 2012.

Lipton, Bruce H. *The Biology of Belief: Unleashing the Power of Consciousness, Matter & Miracles*. Hay House, 2016.

MULFORD, PRENTICE. *THOUGHTS ARE THINGS*. SUBLIME Books, 2018.

Murphy, Joseph. *The Power of Your Subconscious Mind: the Complete Original Edition, plus Bonus Material*. St. Martin's Essentials, 2019.

NIGHTINGALE, EARL. *STRANGEST SECRET: How to Live the Life You Desire*. SIMPLE TRUTHS LLC, 2020.

JW Rucker Jr.

Rafai, Jamal-un-Nisa Bint. *Quran*. Ta-Ha Publrs.

Seyfarth, Heinrich. *Buddah*. Rose, 1913.

Wilson, Willie F. *Releasing the Power within through Spiritual Dynamics: The Genius of Jesus Revealed*. House of Knowledge, 2000.

Acknowledgments

I am grateful for being a created and creative expression of the Infinite One Source of Power (God, Universe, Quantum field, etc.) that is ever present in me. I thank my wife Adrianne for her unconditional love and inexhaustible kindness as I worked through this book. I would like to thank my four daughters for their kind words, encouragement, and inspiration.

JW Rucker Jr.

About the Author

JW Rucker Jr. Is an retired educator, and ministry leader. A rare heart condition forced him into retirement in 2010. For a while JW suffered from anxiety and depression as it related to the loss of what He loved to do. However, after discovering how the power of thought could help him reinvent himself. He became a can-am Spyder rider, voice actor, author, and public speaker. JW loves to share his story about personal transformation in the midst of crisis and the art of not giving-up. Visit his website- www.alignurmind.com

- Published works-Align Living Life on Purpose

- Host of Align Living Live on Purpose (the Podcast)

- JW holds a bachelor's degree in Criminal Justice and a master's degree in Educational Leadership.

- JW Aspires to work with thought leaders like Dr. Joe Dispenza and others to help people create a better version of themselves.

- JW resides in Georgia with his wife and youngest of four daughters.

END

www.ingramcontent.com/pod-product-compliance
Lightning Source LLC
Chambersburg PA
CBHW060159070426
42447CB00033B/2225